MAMMAL

ANA MARÍA CABALLERO

POETRY

stb
STEEL TOE BOOKS
est. 2003

Cover art by Nancy Baker Cahill
Cover design by John Contreras

ISBN 978-1-949540-40-6
LCCN 2022952047

Steel Toe Books
steeltoebooks.com

For special discounted bulk purchases, please contact sales@steeltoebooks.com

MAMMAL

CONTENTS

I

II

III

For my mother
and daughter

1.

I am tired of the children,
I am tired of the laundry,
I want to be great.

— Sharon Olds

MAMMAL

The hunger strategy is not working ::

Starving the home   as I am starved

Better to serve it   as I am wrought
Bathe it   as I am dowsed
Clothe it   as I am clung

To retort
                 as if dumb

O, something somewhere has ended ::

But not here where my   middle spawns a soul

Watch me sit   while my gut constructs bone
Hear me speak   while my trunk accretes brain
Think me filled   while my belly builds tongue
I transform—yes—transform   stupor

                 into skull

ONE NIGHT I GOT LAID GOT THICK

became a mother

a helpless child's sole object of   desire

a tyrant who apportions joy
a standard of *No*
a fucker up of childhoods

of teenagehoods
of adulthoods
of marriages and their brood

the White shadow in the family portrait
the Confession that finally   comes

all because_

O, sweet sabotage

apology & want

NO LOVER

I am no lover in his bed ::

> Here's the thing: desire as problem
> brings me to me.
> A pregnant married woman,
> thirty-three.

I am no lover in my bed ::

> Perhaps (horribly): my shape.
> (I am shaped like heap.)
> A shape problematic, enigmatic
> for participant mate to fuck.

I am no lover in our bed ::

> Perhaps (predictably): a baby with eyes
> lies inside.
> It's not like it can see us, but baby
> has eyes.

I am no lover in the bed ::

> I can freely say "fuck" because the work
> of procreation,
> of grace, is done.

> Married, my problem of sex, a problem
> for more bodies
> than one.

TRANSMISSION (VARIATIONS IN *A*)

There are 1,109 words that begin with *ana*. This is because *ana* is a Greek root, one that means *on, up, through*. *Ana* makes other words, other roots, go above and beyond. Like *anaphora*, like *anabasis*, like *anagram*, like *anachronism*.

The translation of *ana* in English is *per*. As in per-son. Which I was instructed comes from the Latin *personare*—to sound through—which in turn comes from Roman theater. From actors on stage whose echoes had to puncture costume, pierce mask, to declare. History's irony, rich, to name as self the wearer of a fabricated face.

If there is one etymology to remember, it is that of *person*.

If there is a second etymology to remember (for me) it is *ana*. *Ana* as root, as enterprise of *anatomy*—the body above and beyond the naming of parts.

But *ana* as personal name does not emerge from its function as Greek root. Rather, from the Hebrew and Arabic word for *grace*. Derivations, history's descendants of *Hannah*, palindromic, like *Ana*. Pervasive, like grass. Even in tongues read through Cyrillic, the two open-throat vowels, the temperate consonant clamor. *Ah. N-ah.*

Of course, after all the eons of saying, of naming, it's only natural—we ran out of words, out of sounds; we doubled up.

Ana as grace; *ana* as root. Animal communication is the transmission of information via sound, sight, smell, touch. *Ah. N-ah.* What raw need is met by this call?

Grace—above and beyond.

On a full moon night, I teach my four-year-old girl to howl. She howls *ahuuuuu*. Remembers now, upon moon sight, to howl. A transmission that communicates.

Hums of *a* followed by echoes of *u*—that petit *a* hurled out as you.

CORD

It's tricky to understand the relation
between the boy that rockets my days
and the baby that balloons my midsection.

Between the father who falters in a distant location
and the brother who deliberately strays.
Between the push of the conduit, the live construction

inside, which feeds a fetus after conception,
and the pull that sucks meconium away.
These links so tricky but not like, I think, incantations

such as precede red scarf, white bird transmutation—
no gloved, swift, skilled hands at play.
Only, once everyone inside tied—intimate communication:

now, everyone outside untied—yet roped by correlation.
Your daughter, sister, mother. Your covey.
Yours as in *federal*, wide rights, packed implications.

For my baby to exit my womb, I'll require a c-section—
gloved, swift, skilled hands will fray
a literal cord, an umbilical connection.
What remains is so tricky, fabricated words of relation.

LINNAEUS

More botanist than poet, he was, decidedly.

A namer—inventor of systems of pinning unknowns, observed
unknowns. From the broad to the small—the explicit.

A namer in parts, not only of being
but of type. Mammals he defined as class, as partition.
Rank, category, limit.

Binomial brand.

He had seven children. Imagine his wife, Sara. Scrubbing
their offspring's skin

Their seven *homo sapiens*:

Carl
Elisabeth Christina
Sara Magdalena
Lovisa
Sara Christina
Johannes
Sophia

Was Lovisa the gentle-mannered? Sophia, the youngest,
was she the vague? Did Sara recover
from baby Sara Magdalena's,
from Johannes' deaths?

And firstborn Carl, what did he inherit
from his father, the annotator, the divider,
the decider of names?

Poet-botanist, creature-cartographer, ceremony-gardener.

One being, one
witness.

One universe as range.

CUSTODIAL

It is the child who establishes the legality of war

The child   who begets parents
          out of mere partner mere
                    spouse
                              who renders a couple
Custodial
                              who ends reign of mother's
mother & father's father

          The child
who by absolute need   commands its makers to reiterate

          the domestic clamor

                              of spoil

MAMMAL FOURTEEN

perhaps it stops being about
      us loving us

& more about
ceasing
          embracing a life that ends

      watch   it   end

i bought flimsy pajamas   for you
              for me
                    for us

     lace for the children's
          rock-hard home

       but who cares about sex
i just want you to wipe away baby shit

mature love   is the best

     it makes you smarter
     because you have to think

i've always preferred smart   to happy
our mid-life love makes me   happy

    i think

WEEK THIRTY-NINE: PLACENTA

Man with ultrasound wand
says baby is losing weight—

We must take your baby out,
I will call your doctor, tell her
to induce you tomorrow.

Outside the room, my doctor
and wand man are husband
and wife, his call one of groceries,
of take out dog, of pick up kid,
and wait,
before I forget.

Are you sure? I ask.
I feel so well,
baby inside me
feels so well.

This is not a thing you'd sense,
see, here—
plain as clear cold gel.

Take mine. Reference it.

My placenta stopped
working.

No food
for my firstborn,

such physical failure
a not uncommon thing.

MAMMALIAN CREATURES—

- Are endothermic vertebrates
  - This means spines prod inside
- Have hair and fur on exterior of the body
  - This means protection from menace of surface
- Have sebaceous, sudoriferous, and scent glands
  - Literacy of the solid, of the liquid, discerning of the gas
- Have heterodont dentation
  - Sharpness and occasion honed
- Have a diaphragm
  - This means mastery of suck via sack of lung
- Have one single jawbone
  - Vernacular process of chew
- Have three small bones in the middle of the ear
  - This means balance and capacity to hunt on quadruple or duplicitous foot
- Have mammary glands
  - This means breast but not necessarily attached to chest
- Have four-chambered hearts
  - Hearts augmented, beat divided

A.D.

Cold front in Miami
Vapor whorls on moving lips

The ocean heaves dragon green
Turns against its shore

After drop-off I join the mothers
To presage a harvest moon

We amass as gatherers
On days when hunting looms

MAMMARY

What defines us is the breast.

Suckle of   milk   from   gland of lend.
        True life   from   true give.

Linnaeus coined in 1758:
mammal, from *mammalia*, neuter plural of Late Latin *Mammalis*, "of the
breast," cognate with *mamma*, cognate with *mama*.

        Kindred, of the same material kind. Of the young who suckle.
        Newly born, warm-blooded
                air   breathers.

All creatures have a mother. Are reptiles not mothers?
A salamander has a mother. A bird with nest is mother.

        Though birds:
                are they unlike by virtue of flight
                and subsequent faculty
                            of sovereign eye?

Untrue life: is
fish reproduction better termed
fish self-division? Is there just one
fish? One single
fish fished?

The event of mother
hooks and
un   hooks
mamma
from child.

MUJERES

My toddler daughter and grandmother like to doze off together to the sound of TV after lunch.

Just look at them—napping on the tarmac grey couch.

Nina in her yellow Journey t-shirt and whimsy-printed panties, face down, occupying space like dropped cutlery.

Estelita guards her posture. You'd hardly suspect she snores (though she does). Positioned in the corner like a minor museum artifact—the kind none would bother to re-catalogue.

I watch them from the kitchen counter while I sip soup and answer emails with a wrung spine:

Yes. Okay. But first.

The movie playing on TV—*La isla de las mujeres*—a 1953 black and white Mexican film Estelita found on Univisión. The movie's unreal world is governed by women: men are forced to pound clothes clean, soothe bellowing babies, pulverize thick-shelled spices via muscle and mortar.

Naturally, they—the men—rebel.

Three out of four generations of my family's women occupy the realm of my kitchen. Estelita, ninety something (of her years no one is certain), left an alcoholic husband in Colombia to raise six children alone in South Florida. My mother, nearly seventy, tends to my father, whose mind was swallowed by a drunken slip. And I, forty, winching two companies from the abyss of my brother's avarice.

I cannot recall Nina as a baby, I tell you—cannot.

I rise to turn the TV off, but don't. Instead, I take my place between the resting bodies and watch the men revolt.

2.

Out the window snow is falling down in straight lines. To my
mother,

 love
of my life, I describe what I had for brunch.

—Anne Carson

PARENTAGE

Ana, mother of María. María, mother of Jesus. Jesus, son of María. María, daughter of Ana. Ana, grandmother of Jesus. Jesus, grandson of Ana. Parentage is linear and circular and perpendicular always intersecting related physical bodies at once.

Ana and *María*, through time, merged into a commonly given name, my name. As name, grandmother and mother conjoin into singular oracular vernacular form: free of son, oh, that omniscient, eternally suffering son.

Ana María. Not, Ave María.

In Spanish, grandmother does not translate into *gran-madre*. Not grand cognate idiom of mother but a construct all its own, exact, *abuela*. My *abuelas* are Estela and Lucía. Lucía, *Lula,* died at age 102 and ran a dairy farm on the outskirts of Bogotá until shortly before she passed. Estela, *Estelita,* whose name traced to source means *star,* still drives and lies about her age. Because of my parentage, I am led to believe I may never die.

I go by *Ana,* which means I twist my neck when this word is said: *Ana. Ana* built of two *a*'s one *n*. Latin *Ana.* Nothing eternally suffering about the uttering of this name.

The compound name *Ana María* too much toil in my mouth, your mouth—too beholden to mother, my mother, to lineage.

You see: my mother's name is *Ana María,* too. Specifically, *Ana María de la Auxiliadora,* the name Estela, *Estelita,* promised the Virgin Mary to give her fourth child if it was born a girl after she pushed out three live boys.

Ave María. The Virgin delivered.

Auxilio means *Help!*—the exclamation necessary to translation. *Help! me Virgin,* Virgensita, *send me a girl. If you do, I will name her like you,* María Auxiliadora.

I go sit stand as *Ana*. So slight no one suffers when it is uttered. So self-contained it shrugs all familial weight. Neutral yet familiar, secular in its generational faith.

My daughter shoulders her own name. No need to break to be free. I am her mother, sure, an axle of story, but not the atlas, not her cardinal system of way.

Nina, I named her. *Nina Isadora. Go on*, with my muzzle I nudge her, *go on and be great.*

WEEK SEVENTEEN: BEHOLDEN

Even though I am not funny,
my son laughs.

His laughter does not make me   feel
                                 funny
but beholden—

like I owe him a joke now;
like I better get funny soon;
before he is old enough to remark—

      mommy is not   funny.

But somber—

      a string pulled from its spool into a snap horizon.

You need not drop your gaze:
                                 if it becomes hard to see me,
I will be the first to say,

          turn away.

CONCEPTUAL AGE

Since worm seed in
round, buoyant egg.

Not to be confused
with gestational age—
before seed grabs
egg.

Time since
body first thinks
to prepare. To
procure.

Conceptually,
we're younger.

An idea
newer to this world.

FIRST BORN

How am I supposed to sleep
when I give birth to-   morrow?

Sleep now because
you will never sleep   again,
the erstwhile pregnant mothers   claim.

Never shall I state such a fruitless   thing
to a woman swelling   life

with this newness
who gets   hungry
and has a cry at   night.

MAMMAL TWELVE

Me breed baby be

Me eat baby sprout

Me sit baby swim

Me bend baby ball

Me stretch baby spread

Me drink baby drain

Me sleep baby kick

Me wait baby gain

Me break baby born

THIS HOLDING

I finally understand how forever works:

One day, you had a wife, had sex, got her pregnant, had a daughter.
One day, I was wife, had sex, got pregnant, birthed a daughter.
One day.

One day, you were harried. Industrious hands shaking hands.

One day and another.

Those days are not today, are not these days, those days are done days.

But one day and another, industrious harried hands shaking other
hands, not holding daughter.

One day and another, mother at start, at end of day, enfolded by
daughter.

That one day, that other day, are not today.

But these hands.

This holding.

UNRAVELING

As mom, I became writer,
present yet   removed,
notably in the afternoons.

Now he is three—
descends
         full
                  flights
                           of stairs,
                           selects
                  the word
         for where
it hurts.
Wooden blocks knocked
                  down

                  again.

Again, I am late for pick-up.

He jumps and shouts of what
he played while I—
I wrote about the new baby
unraveling
my inside.

It's hard to say.

I allow
it
         to hover,
         the word
for
where
      — for if—
it hurts.

MAMMAL SEVEN

Life latches
The host succumbs
    Collapsed in sleep
        Gravity of spawn
            Blood gluts vein
                The future as frame

My teeth gnaw
To stock the spore
    God funds us as one
        Selfsame cave
            A single curl upon the bed
                Combined drained weight

No sport to employ
My young animate boy
    No mattress wife
        I am loamy mass
            Fecundity worms
                Below my belt

INTERNAL COMBUSTION

We take turns.

Mine last night to be done.
Today it is yours.

When it's your turn, I feel bad and overdo
to make you feel good.
In this manner, I become done, again, too soon.

We are ordinary: our marriage, like many, a mid-century
            internal combustion engine—
by piston and pressure gears shift forward,
            bearings of moderate, unsteady locomotion.

Friction derives from overuse.

Like how now you gesture for me to leave her—
leave the girl untended while I try to write this.

(Do you know it's about you and plot
for me to write you kind?)

But it's hard for us mothers to be unfun,
to unwind flat like a busted slide—
and I get angry at you because I can't.

(Don't you see I need
        our girl to love me kind?)

All this love wanting love.

Pistons thrust, impelled by scorched oil.
Filthy fuel—mean summary of past decay.

Yet, this resource remains source:

it powers, propels, allows us to go.
      Also, to nurse—run the motor low.

We consume energy,
invent ways to ignore
its dirtying burn.

MAMMAL SIX

Children, we have.

Sex, we've had.

Blueprints tell us where the bedroom hangs.

What more can come of love?

The way its doors swing in, hinged.

I reside, dwell, abide, identify each object by its drawer.

To enter the space of home is to house, to hold. To wed, to lock.

Young survive better if two adults watch.

But if biology is the circuitry inside, how so my lashing out?

Every day blows its bit of wind.

See the doors: still: they beckon in.

IF FEMALE, THE BODY PREPARES

for the possibility of child—builds walls of sustenance, cushions of clay.

Quiet as grotto,

awaits insemination, conceivable fertilization—the shuffle of nucleic matter we

sort as epithet:

discreet, thick, slight, brave. Though we absorb them as custom, as culture, the syndromes

of our organs'

labors result not from endeavor but from fact—blood runs down the inner thigh

of a grown

girl. Once I spot red, I can claim I've lived enough, seen enough, to come of age:

to walk as

latter lady, little woman, ripened daughter. My girl mind, my girl soul, lime green mangos

fallen—ovular in their form.

THE WISH

To coexist with the male I love, I train in embrace of emotional shove.
His life expends before three large screens. I'm no match
for their shiny black grins.

Yet, love as crave disinterests me: I dream in ascetic walkways
at the end of which I find I love myself enough
for both of us.

Meanwhile, a hurricane the size of South Florida approaches South
Florida: South Florida
is home.

I buy water, think of places to go if we must evacuate. Husband sits.
Do we stay or leave? Will power go out? We have small children.
Husband wants to read.

Low pressure systems may send hurricane north, toward other
homes—that terrible wish.

Congress without, no wind within.

We wait.

Wish the awful wish.

WEEK FOUR: NATIVITY

The method of delivery defines
the type of mammal we, they, you,
are. The category of creature I am.

They are monotreme, they who are reptilian,
birdlike in their method of birth. A cracked
white shell announces their first day.

Monotremes possess cloacas — one canal
to expel excrement, urine, and the egg
that descends from within to scheme without.

You are marsupial, you who clamber
undeveloped into your momma's pocket.
Out of differentiated birth canal you arrive

to climb incomplete into her warm pelted
pouch. No one blames you
for this extra time inside.

I who am placental — food and waste
conveyed via same-serving, cloaca-like rope.
Then, cord sliced, tied: belly button bulge.

Initially conjoined, I was cut free upon first breath
alive. An entire lifetime spent nursing
such self-determining slice.

DESIRE

Efficient my wrists   they   open
        and   sort our   mail

       (it once made me sad to masturbate)

Fearsome my arms   they   bag
        and   haul out   trash

       (that original time around)

Deliberate my feet   they   sweep
        and   pick up   crumbs

       (but now that I am again saddled with child)

Systemic my hips   they   bear
        and   hoist small   tykes

       (there is no lament no disgrace)

Formidable my fists   they   spread
        and   knead the   dough

       (convinced routine carves space)

Aquatic my hands   they   soak
        and   rinse round   plates

       (I drill what he won't fill)

Tactical my knees   they   clean
        and   cross our   hearth

       (spurred to discover my articulate core)

33

I wonder what will become of me in terms of basic living when I become a living poet. Like will it make me free of the moms. Like on the days when I wake up feeling fabulous those days (I confess only here) are really not scarce those days when I wake and want to hug my incredible body with color and sparkle and mismatch my hems because you see I am silly in private but never in public or hardly at sunset and slide plastic pearls into my hair and drop off my children looking too fabulous for Tuesday or so I am told by the looks of the moms and by looks I don't mean eyes inside sockets but exclusivity transmitted by clothes. But it's okay that I'm off being fabulous because I write poems that get published so I am able now also to drop off children and pick up children and attend Halloween Thanksgiving Easter cake table elementary parties looking like shit on the days when I feel like shit those days (I confess only here) are really not scarce and my visible shittiness owned by my face and worn by my body and the moms will know I am writing a lot of poems that get published. Like this I wonder will I be free of one thing.

And I wonder too if I will become able to speak to the moms when they arrange themselves into their saying circles and talking triangles and speaking squares but mostly the circles will I too be able to stay in the sense that I'll be cleared to stand silent as in no words alleged by my lavender tongue when chat turns to things I can't grip for the extended moments required for discussion like the comparative value of similar things because I never learned to talk quality talk for more than one swing. Will I be passed over when it's my turn but permitted to stay because I'm that mom who's an avowedly awkward writer of poems that get published. Like this I wonder will I belong to one thing.

And when I have books that are printed with words of things I literally said because I thought them then wrote them and my thoughts will be there will be here will reveal that it's so communal really so extant in circles this wish to belong along with this need to be free. Free of the moms but hatched by the moms burrowed deep in the warmth of their globular caverns of say and by writing this will I swathe with verse the singlemindedness with which their children are tended and school functions attended. Like this I wonder will I conquer one fear.

And when I say all these things (and by say you know I mean write) will I transmit something more than this blow of me and forty right now here where I sit a woman of forty right now with the face and the gait and the buckled belt the buckled child and this this this buckled awe of a mom.

WAITING ROOM

Twenty-six weeks ago, you entered my belly as an invisible coin.
Now I bump into walls with your bulge,
spill soup on you,
prop my elbows across your arched loins.
Nina, our space is this—
this one evening as minute in a moonlit room.
I invite you to take over as you do,
exhaust me as you do.
Fourteen more weeks,
child,
to crowd my organs flat,
to know absolute privacy,
to witness the secret of my swollen eye,
to collect my voice with the web of your hands.

tú, yo, tuyo

Only once will I allow you to see this, Nina—
this one collapse by the cage of your crib.
Is my shaking waking you?
Don't think it common:
it is just the waiting that does this.
Not for you—
no.
I wait for me.
For the mother in me to take care of me.
To birth me and bathe me and put me to sleep,
here,
in your room—where the moon primes my womb,
so I may rise to receive you,
reliable as a worn wooden spoon.

3.

Ah,
to make them invisible,

to no longer hear the
       demands
of their flesh as
       commands

more pressing, more powerful
       than those
which come from
       mine.

—Elena Ferrante

WORDS OF CONNECTION

he spoke:

you expect me to be home like a mom
you want me to be home in the morning in the evening
both days of the weekend
i want to be great but because of you i can't

i study the words
signs dialed by husband's
mind that quit his throat as waves
drilling sound into my head

(what exactly did he say
what exactly did i hear)

my response is vicious
silence

(waveless firearm)

am i angry do i love less
so long as he picks up kids
do i care
what noise his mouth makes

(my muteness turns to wonder
for i too am a body
who contemplates fame)

constriction around
sternum with gag
fixed in pharynx

we stagger up
same snaked
ziggurat
toward great

WEEK SEVEN: THE WAY

This is the way I cut the grass:

> Green limbs
> We tug
> You yank / I haul

This is the way I fill the tub:

> I forget the bubbles
> Water structures
> My limpid bath

This is the way I name my files:

> No comfort is found in your mouth
> My problems are earned
> I am a poor navigator of life
> Ask for more / you take the bone
> Your job to slate / mine to record

This is the way I pour the milk:

> Having kids is hard
> Having kids is effing hard
> I no longer say fuck
> Or fucking hard

I administer home:

> Yet remain
> Secretary of the board

BROTH PRAYER

Dear God,

Please remove my mother.

Keep her far from my blithe breakfast light.

She is the drain. I am the broth.

Whisk me in my copper pot.

Amen

BOY CHILD

this child i wash every night
sleeps
by my side
bad parenting i am told

the child is bathed
washed cotton clothed
fed and drained from play
close to me
touching me
telling me it loves me
a friend says *i have a manual*
that can help

the child (a boy) calls me *mimi*
like the chorus from the drake song

you can't sleep here forever, i caution
only now
and every single night daddy is gone

the boy child its bad
morning breath no mouthwash rinses clean

the boy child kicks cries for water
chokes me with the limbs of his taking
demands we read about black holes
pluto's planetary status
the brain's limited knowledge of itself

i do everything it says
convinced i want it too

this book this baby they say
let the boy child stay
for tomorrow's big legs race
men children away

VASECTOMY (AN INCISION IN PARTS)

For M.M.

I: Perform Objective Observation

I swallow birth control pills for seventeen years
until one day my body tells me to stop, I swear it spoke,
begged me—enough.

I deliver our firstborn son alone via emergency c-section
in a glacial operating room after his heartrate drops
during induced contractions of birth.

I breastfeed our insatiable boy despite torn
nipples and a nipple stone—
like a kidney stone, so.

Another cesarean to birth our girl,
then months hunched over as wet-nurse.

For five years I ask patiently, incessantly: *Love, go get it done.*

He says: *Why should I put my body through that when condoms work fine?*

Twelve years of marriage, five years of courtship—
and here I am, freezing mid-coupling for rubber,
inspecting damp latex post-coitus.

He almost fifty, I almost forty—
both of us still laden with dreams.

Methodically, we do not want more kids.

II: Ask Questions

If the condom rips, below are the possible outcomes to this:
Morning after pill—
Whereby I dial the doctor,
I haul to a pharmacy,
I gulp hormones. I put
my body through that.

A child—
Of course, we will love the cute little baby,
but what happens at night, when it needs to eat,
and my husband thinks he can sleep?

An abortion—
An abortion.

III: Construct a Hypothesis

All the above outcomes, eventually, lead to this:

I demolish my husband—
Because he responds in kind, in due
course, he will wreck me back.

The end—
The two kids we love and have raised,
our marriage with its professional sex,
and look at us, every day, better friends.
All of it ends.

IV: Test the Predictions

I sit him down. Sketch out the end
using paper and pen.

Inside my head, I encounter Lysistrata,

44

so I say: *No sex until—snip, snip.*

After three weeks, he gets the gist,
finally goes to the urologist.

V: Is the Experiment Working?

Four years ago, he had a testicular infection.

Since then, two—maybe three—times,
he's suffered a bit of bother
down there.

The urologist decrees a chronic condition,
scribbles a note my husband brings home:

Not advisable to make an incision.

VI: Troubleshoot Procedure

I convey my findings to my colleague María,
who provides key insights:

Before my second c-section,
my husband told my male gyno—
            doctor, can you tie her tubes
            when you slice her?

But, Maria, doesn't that make recovery
much more painful?

Have you ever seen a man
not have a woman take the hit
for a man? Suck it up. Secure your reproduction.
What about that hormone-free copper T
that is pushed into the uterus?

VII: Analyze

I want to stay married to the same man.
Condoms are depressing.
Holy shit no more kids.

     I get the gist.
     I call my gynecologist.

VIII: Use Experimental Data as Background for New Procedure

On the day the copper apparatus is inserted
I say: *Honey, don't forget my appointment today.*
Wait, he moans, *you want me to go?*

It's in your calendar, I affirm, *the procedure will hurt.*
But I have a call.

My first period after insertion, I bleed streams for ten days.
In the bathroom, I point to the torrents of red.

Jesus, he cries.
The internet said this might happen, I groan.
Oh, so it's normal, he sighs.

     I experiment with observable nonreaction
     in favor of result-based results.

IX: Draw Conclusions

I need to bleed through a maxi tampon,
if I want to control my outcome.

X: Report Findings

I cold-store every implicit word
within the scientific body of this poem,

which one day will land,
unapologetic as consequence,
upon his hairy heterosexual hand.

BAD AND WOLFING

The problem of it is the bullshit.

Bad behavior brings consequence, I warn,
no TV, no candy.

Yet here I am: bad and wolfing. *I am serious.*
I will count to three. My vehemence awful

as the truth of awfulness.

May my children chew with closed jaws, give thanks,
quit throwing mulch at the park. Beyond that—

what? Above is my mother,
her errors toward me eolic: at times a gust,

at others a squall.
O, but doth each visit blow.

Below is my daughter. Between us
me and my erroneous storms of constancy.

We reveal each other—a play within a play,
a cloud within a lake. If I was Italian,

I would utter, *circolo.* No exit from the cycle
that traps us like wet weather.

I will not prevent the tempest
by forcing my daughter to wear a sweater—

still, I make her.

NOT THE LIFE I DREAMED

is not an effective way to say—

this is not
the life I dreamed.

Preferable to deliver
such meaning abstractly,

from the distant clean of metaphor:

the curt, indigo waves
of Lake Okeechobee
veil drifting alligators well.

Honey,
I love you.

You are a terrific father,
a terrific man.

My nipples are bleeding
from feeding our baby.

That is all.

MAMMAL THIRTY-NINE

Most day long I want myself.
Of course, I'll say, *Hi!* I'll say, *Hey.*
Hey.
But truly, fully, I crave myself—
my roles, my waves.
Except for there are times
I lack a fuck,
not with myself
but with another—
a farther, further, self.
And because of how,
exactly,
I occur:
with my exact husband man.
Hi! I'll say,
wanna fuck?
Sure, he'll go,
let's fuck.
You see, most day long
he, too, craves himself—
his doingness, his tasks.
Except for when he lacks
his woman wife,
which is me,
exactly:
Hey! I'll say back,
even though
I don't really get
this need to fuck—
that spasm of hunger
for peripheral self—
and fail to grasp
how desire births bodies
that occupy
entire continents:

billions of farther,
further,
internally exact selves
who lack
as want.

MILK

At first, infants love us for our colostrum.

A few days later and perhaps for months, our milk.

Eventually, though, children love us for nothing.

My children love me for nothing.

Define nothing: the breadth between caregiving and caretaking.

I never forget to call my mother whom I remember to never forgive.

My children cry when I leave their sight, though I invent alleyways through which to depart.

And yet: I'm most myself when I'm alone, pressing hard against my sleeping child.

Define alone: a mass of uncut bread.

Or else: the bellow of a cow at dawn.

Meanwhile, my children's range, their capacity, expands.

I hold pictures of them as babies and cannot recall their size upon my breast.

Was I there?

As a youth, I scuttled through alleyways to escape my mother's hearth.

I hurt from loving too much and not enough.

Time leaves my sight.

What I cannot stand about my mother is the way she reminds me of myself.

Am I here?

I have never been this old.

CESAREAN

I was sliced open twice to yield two lives. The doctor who cut
the second time traced the lines of the first.

She said: *This is where you open, and this is where you close.*
This is where I carve, and this is where I sew.

I asked: Doctor, *can I deliver naturally?* Her answer: *Well—yes.*
But there's always a risk that the first slash will rip.

I love the way birthing makes the body mean. Via gore,
immortality.

My friends say I am lucky. They say my husband is lucky.
They laugh. It's hilarious that my vagina, at forty, is still tight.

I'm so tired of professing verve in the face of it all. All means the truth,
that numerical lore.

If youth is the promise of fruit, why clutch with no crop left
to yield?

Sex in the house is noiseless, purloined—devout in its efforts
to shield innocuous kids.

I bite my slice of layer cake. Its technicolor dough tastes sweet,
but I spit.

Though famished, my pharynx only swigs fuel
that sinks.

MAMMAL ONE

It is done
The baby grows
Silent as a new world

I must consider it
When I eat
Eat more

Again
I am thirsty
Again

It is the baby
Already telling me
What to do

PENCIL DRAWING

Forgive this bare poem,
but it is about emptiness—
which I suppose could be outlined
in a colorful way—
but I am trying to be honest,
like Hemingway, who said his books were one true phrase
after the next:
rows of letters reaching for no more
than the direction towards which they flow—
arrows, markers, tombstones.

For all my living, I am but a small vertical line:
I
go nowhere—
trapped between the thought above
and the thought below—
like a dash.

Do you see my tidy body hunched
atop a keyboard in the quiet coffee shop?

Witness my hands
not typing the report owed my job;
my throat not answering
my grandmother's repeated call;
my face not smiling for strangers
at the counter; my bandaged toe, broken
while furiously picking up children's clothes.

Will you remember any of it?

How I held my breath
and wrote,
how I possessed such few words,
how my lungs were hungry vagrant sacs,

how once I was as empty
as I was alive.

i'm a different woman in every room   in the kitchen efficient   operative as fork   quiet in
the bedroom   tiptoe to avoid discourse   the weight of telling you everything is fine   nothing
happened   in the bathroom confessional   thoughts bend into curve hungry as the dip
that concludes my spine   the volume of forward   of woman who stays   in the nursery
nostalgic   i summon the past   a love of distant animals   whales   i recall a birth
in the city   but corridors and orbits circle me further   back to a village fit for a child   to music
recitals   where grandmothers pace with wet hair   and always a radiola walls argentine
protest songs   in the living room watchful   caution girdles my methods   i observe the
strawberry i drop on the floor upon which another might slip everything is hardwood   formica
shelves new but coated in dust   parked in the driveway generous   i prepare the wits and
gifts to present believe i will sleep unaided   formless and flexible   like the babe in my belly
like the shape of my tongue about to commit   no one is lonelier than the woman who is loved

FRUITION

There must be a right way to chop cauliflower,
one that doesn't spew a million tiny florets
all over the kitchen counter like so many clots
of beige blood bursting from a zero-gravity
wound, you see, I have this problem whereby
I can't stand mess anymore—which is a problem
because Emerson says it's a problem, this need
of my mind to categorize though I can't help the despair
I feel (which must look like rage to my children)
when I see burnt turmeric all over the stove before
sitting down to eat—I know what you're thinking—
why not heat up tortillas, but I have this other
problem, which is I crave tikka masala every
week, and that's a problem because Goethe
says it's a problem, this need of my mind to live
full at all cost, so I mince ginger and onion though
the skins and rinds drive me nuts, even crazier,
I'll over-sprinkle cumin and coriander until they jet
out of the pan (because, come on, live a little)
but then immediately I must sponge it up, so I
wonder if I'm the secret villain from a Telemundo
soap opera who won't just chill and grill tortillas,
but instead must wreck the lives of other people—
here "other people's lives" a metaphor for tikka
masala (but you got that, of course)—and the mess
in my kitchen isn't so bad as the rush in my brain
to tidy it up, not as bad as how my opposing problems
collide: my desire for explosive mixtures of spices
(bang!) against my obsession for impeccable counters—
now you see why I must turn and return to Linnaeus,
who tells me it's fine to catalog every crumb,
while I concoct a categorically unsortable life.

ANCESTRY

For Estelita

"Your great grandfather, Don Lorenzo Botero, had eighteen children. His wife, Mamá Carolina, was pregnant for nearly twenty years. Lorenzo, the son, your grandfather, my ex-husband, had seventeen brothers and sisters. Of which he knew.

Don Lorenzo, the father, used to ride his horse from Sonsón in Antioquia to Pereira in Risaralda. Back and forth, a beautiful man on his beautiful horse. He, a *señor.* Not a *señorito.*

The story goes that between Sonsón and Pereira whosoever was not the child of Don Lorenzo was the child of his horse."

"But *abuela* Estelita," I asked, "did Mamá Carolina know?"

"Know? Oh, I guess so," Estelita said, amid laughter, amid giggles. "But can you just imagine, being pregnant for twenty years?"

This story, its laughter, is the answer to any question I posed of Lorenzo, the son—Estelita's ex-husband—my mother's father. An alcoholic who as a figure nevertheless emerges historic—the founder of Colombia's National Merchant Association. Was it an aunt, an uncle, my mother, who once told me that founding anything is a drinking business?

Baroque, florid.

Estelita left him in the Sixties. One day, when pressed, she confessed: "He drank everything, I needed money, so I left. Traveled alone from Bogotá to South Florida with six children. We moved in with a cousin. Got jobs. Dairy Queen. Howard Johnson's. Jordan Marsh. Rough? Yes, I suppose it was rough."

Florid, humid, torrid. Never did Estelita conjure horrid.

When I begged for history, she countered with lore—the progeny of her father-in-law and his horse. Don Lorenzo, a punctum, despite his passing back and forth. The elusive señor reclaimed as reverie by a woman who built her own myth to rejoice in its slips.

WEEK NINETEEN: DAY OF THE MOTHER

I remind the one
Who is my husband
To bring a small gift soon
It will be the Day of the Mother
Role of Father Man
Husband Male
To procure
Offering
Box
For me to undo
I tell him I am pliable
I point to trivial things
Explain how to go
He says he thought
Of something better
But he does not
Did not
Go
Am I sad
Am I literally sad
Am I sad poem sad
Am I proven right sad
Am I things will never change sad
Am I validator of bipartisan role of Mother
Sad
Mother's Day w/o box
W/o compensation
W/o plastic balloon
W/o breakfast on tray
W/o single drugstore rose unthorned
W/o picture to prove
To post to prove
Do I care
Do I want to care
Do I make myself care

Can I make it stop
Can I forgo
And if not
Can I go out
Can I buy a box
Bag my own goddamn
Reward

DETECTION

*The extremes are easy. Only
the middle is a puzzle.*
Louise Glück

Saramago dreamt of a world awoken blind,
maintaining the problem of those who see
as the problem of something, always, to size.

I type with shut eyes because my brain
memorized where the letters on my keyboard lie.

I open my lids: photons hit my cornea,
pierce my lens—organs primed
for detection, for distraction.
Macula to retina to optical nerve to brain to body—

constant detection as constant disruption.

Again, I seal my gaze and sense: unavailable colors,
the barred beckoning of depth, the death
of one as the immediate disappearance of all.

But all cannot go.

In folding life, my body finds that other-sensing "I"
swathed in pink—not bubble gum,
not flamingo, not guava, not punch—but blush,
the raw shadow at the rainbow's rim,
where red ends and sky begins.

Talk does not last long with father. Bad hand inside plate signals the end of his lucidity respite.

But who says what matters? What is food? What is fed? His clean hands eat. His closed mouth chews.

The waitress takes a picture. I was a waitress plenty of years and never took a picture. If I remember one thing—it was before cell phone pictures. If I remember another—Thanksgiving as a waitress in New York. How I wanted to interrupt the talk of families at tables to insist it was choice.

Father. Just him, just me. The cloth on our table is heavy and white. Just us. I cut his pasta and help him scoop it onto the spoon held by his good hand. He attempts to ask about my kids. But the sentence goes adrift, is annulled, swallowed. No matter.

His bad hand enters his plate. I clean it with a paper napkin. Request others.

Bad hand, baffled sentence. Sudden but familiar face of permanent surprise. His pool blue eyes empty as water. Water that would say.

When he finishes, again, I clean his hands.

Dialogue is the thing when a matter goes forth and back.

VIRGINITY

You were a sort of blood
mother to me: first you held me
close, for eighteen years, and then
you let me go.

Sharon Olds, Ode to my Hymen

Was I ever, am I ever, comfortably outside my mother?

Languishing, always. A thin layer swathed around the truth of our non-resemblance, our non-penetration. Me, her daughter, synopsis of her motherhood, tally of her attendance, packaging of her method—ripped open because the gift so deeply hidden inside.

Because I was so well-behaved, the story of my virginity, of its loss, within the confines of my mother's house, beneath the margin of its Spanish roof tiles, above the line of its surveyed grounds, is a story of secret life.

Of course, I never meant to undermine. Under mine—under my own adolescent body an additional young adult body, is all.

Gustavo, Gerardo, Gilberto, what even was his name?

I'll wager Gerardo. No, I'm not sure of the title of this story's secondary character but certain of his crescendo: he in college, I in high school. His hair bleached (this is important). His toothy kind kid grin. That night, like many, we knocked back blue mojitos at Señor Frogs with his gangly Mexican friend, Abelardo. His name, I am sure of.

Gerardo (yes, let's call him Gerardo) drove me home after Señor Frogs closed its doors, crossed the front gate of my mother's concrete block home, entered the wooden frame of my room.

No reason to enter but to enter.

When you broke—you, hymen—when you tore, you gashed other things along the arc of your cut. For one: image of me as virtuous daughter. And more: idea of me as tractable daughter. Gone: notion of me as pageantry daughter.

The minute you cracked, motion of open at my bedroom door.

Me on my mother's bed, after she walked in mid-coitus, trying to explain. *This was only the first time.* Praying, God, please don't let my blood stain her bed. Testimony sealed with a red dragging kiss—scarlet ingredient of plunge—down the inseam of my thigh.

My mother's response, *It's too bad it had to be like this, your first time.* I should've lied. Confessed it to be the fifth, the eighth, the twentieth time.

After that, I tried to hang out with Gerardo, but we were over, done for, invalid. I ashamed, he ashamed, my mother ashamed. All of us, yoked by our communal bath of shame.

Shame in my mother brews anger. My event, her personal offense. By then, I sensed her need to slaughter hurt by lashing out. Daughter a reflection, whose survival a matter of deflection.

Haven't I taught you well, haven't I taught you better?

Yes, mother, the problem, the ruin, is me.

Me, though—her summary.

To move on, I hunted for a deft second time. Quickly, I found it. No need for specifics: *Yeah, I've done it.* Of course, all I'd done was crack you—you—blameless den. All I'd done was bleed your placid cover into my shower. All I'd done was further affix terror and submission, reserve and fascination to the being of mother—that particular soul whose body cooked me and housed me before hurling me out.

I have a daughter now. A daughter with a small daughter hymen, to have and to unhave, to rupture as her interactions deem fit.

At some point, I will speak to her of promise, of pleasure, and of how they can be divorced from puncture. But mostly I yearn for thoughts of me to never pierce her way.

To get my daughter wish, I must first absolve my mother.

All that is sullied within, if not transfigured clean, will seep, pollute, whip out into the world of precious new daughter for whom I want nothing of the righteous shame dispensed by category of mother.

I must reach beyond the hungry comfort of pattern to empty of permission. Become pliant as membrane, a filter of past into present— sieve that does not cleave but bends, gently, to allow the genesis, the sovereign opening of our bloodline's next outbound girl.

VERNACULAR

3:45 pm – After we drop off his cousins at their home after school, my six-year-old son asks the meaning of the word "exquisitely."

3:46 pm—I assume he heard the word from his cousins and invoke gratitude for same-city family and older cousins who will guide him throughout an entirely effective life.

3:47 pm—I ask where he heard the word.

3:48 pm—*In a video.*

3:49 pm—I wallow in small, self-referential mediocre mother thoughts.

3:52 pm   I tell my son what the word means: *In a great, awesome, and incredible way. Okay?*

3:52 pm—*Okay.*

6:07 pm—I drag my son out of soccer class after the class is over but before the last penalty kick is kicked by the last remaining kid.

6:08 pm—I tell him it's been enough, and he's got to learn enough.

6:09 pm—*I hate you exquisitely.*

6:10 pm—Quiet in the car.

6:11 pm—Additional quiet in the car. My son and I both wonder how I, his mother, will react.

6:12 pm—Meanwhile, I, the writer, laugh and turn the music down.

6:13 pm—My son, who does not know me, the writer, does not laugh. He senses a joke he does not get and so assumes the joke is him. Now he must cry because of pride.

6:14 pm—Time for I, the mother, to mother. Impart some valuable lesson about words, harm, and the definition of "enough." But I like I, the writer, better than I like I, the mother, and make the choice to let him cry.

6:15 pm—For a minute.

6:16 pm—While I, the writer, figure out what, exactly, I, the mother, should not say.

6:17 pm—*Exquisitely is the only way to hate your mother. But only your mother. Okay?*

6:17 pm—*Okay.*

MINE

Today is Saturday. I am writing alone
in a hotel room on a Saturday night
because my husband understands that solitude
is a tender gift.

Like now, there are moments
I love him so much,
I cannot conceive him
as mine.

These moments occur when he insists
I go far. From there, I see he remains
my single tunnel across.

Mine, mind, bind.

Loyalty, eventually,
rhymes with *royalty*.
Duty to domain.

It's not duty that sustains
marriage but the mental migration
from curiosity to safe quarter,
the self-replenishing wonder
that a singular person can be *mine*.

In the way that conjugal hums of habitual,
systemic echoes prophecy.

Awe: by constant interface of one
with just one other,
from the habitation of duality:
you who emerges, carved gently,
as if stroked by velvet tassels,
from the walls that confine

each day.

Not *us*, but *I*
from *you*. A frieze
in high relief.

Time. Twined. Mind.

I love you & you
love I.

But only
if by that loving,
I find that I
love I.

THANKS

Mammal is very fortunate to have a lot of mothers.

Its first mother is my daughter, whose birth unraveled me from the inside out and then slowly put me back together—for the wiser, for the better. So many of this book's poems were sketched out while I held her in my arms. Thank you, Nina Isadora, for arriving like a statement of fact. Its second mother is Julie Marie Wade, who read my earliest, disparate pages and insisted that, somehow, they should be amassed into a cohesive whole. Thank you, Julie, for advocating for this book with such conviction that I even believed in it, too. Its third mother, Jan Beatty, took a one-hundred-and-twenty-page manuscript that was trying, as I often do, to do too much and chiseled away with precision and grace. Thank you, Jan, for being *Mammal*'s doula, summarizing it into the material that matters. Then, one fateful evening, Nancy Baker Cahill connected with my words, sparking many, many intimate conversations and a beloved artistic collaboration via which she transformed my poem "If female, the body prepares" into a pulsing, throbbing, magenta womb. Thanks to Nancy, *Mammal* has a magnificent cover, one that beckons the reader deep within its cavernous folds. Finally, no book is born without a publisher. To the team at Steel Toe Books, you've affirmed my work, you've stretched my voice, you've changed my life. Gracias.

ACKNOWLEDGEMENTS

Thank you to the editors of the journals where some of these poems appeared, sometimes in earlier versions:

The Acentos Review: "Fruition," "Mujeres," and "Waiting Room"
Cream City Review: "Virginity"
Gigantic Sequins: "Transmission" (Nominated for a Pushcart Prize)
Mom Egg Review: "Parentage"
Nurture Literary: "Bad and Wolfing" (Nominated for Best of the Net)
Pittsburgh Poetry Journal: "Decline" and "Vernacular"
Playboy Magazine and Sevens Foundation Grant Winner: "Vasectomy: An Incision in Parts"
Portland Review: "room"
Rattle Magazine: "Mammal One"
Salamander: "Milk"
South Dakota Review: "A.D.," "The Wish," "If female, the body prepares," "Mammalian creatures—"
Tiny Journal: "Custodial" and "Mammal Twelve"

ABOUT ANA MARÍA CABALLERO

Ana María Caballero is a Colombian-American literary artist whose work explores how biology delimits societal and cultural rites, ripping the veil off romanticized motherhood and questioning notions that package sacrifice as a virtue. She's the recipient of the Beverly International Prize, Colombia's José Manuel Arango National Poetry Prize, the Steel Toe Books Poetry Prize, a Future Arts Writer Award, a Sevens Foundation Grant and has been a finalist for numerous other literary and arts prizes, including the prestigious Kurt Brown, Vassar Miller, Academy of American Poets Prize and MAXXI Bvlgari Prize in the Digital Sector

The author of six books in Spanish and English, Caballero has presented her poems as fine art at museums and leading international venues, such as the Wroclaw Contemporary Museum, Museo de Arte Miguel Urrutia, bitforms, Office Impart, UNIT, Gazelli Art House and Times Square. She has released digital poems in partnership with TIME, Diario ABC and Playboy and is a contributing writer for Forbes, reporting on what happens when crypto and culture connect.

Widely recognized as a digital poetry pioneer whose own practice is transforming the way language is exhibited, experienced and transacted, she's also the cofounder of Web3 literary gallery theVERSEverse, shortlisted for the Lumen Prize and the Digital Innovation in Art Award.

Learn more about the author at anamariacaballero.com

ANA MARÍA CABALLERO

Printed in the USA
CPSIA information can be obtained
at www.ICGtesting.com
LVHW041943040424
776466LV00019B/35